COUNTING TIME
LIKE PEOPLE
COUNT STARS

COUNTING TIME LIKE PEOPLE COUNT STARS

Poems by the Girls of Our Little Roses,
San Pedro Sula, Honduras

edited by
Spencer Reece

TIA CHUCHA PRESS

ISBN: 978-1-882688-55-5

Book Design by Jane Brunette
Cover and interior photos by Mary Jane Zapp. Used with permission.

PUBLISHED BY:
Tía Chucha Press
A Project of Tía Chucha's Centro Cultural, Inc.
PO Box 328
San Fernando, CA 91341
www.tiachucha.org

DISTRIBUTED BY:
Northwestern University Press
Chicago Distribution Center
11030 South Langley Avenue
Chicago, IL 60628

*Tía Chucha's Centro Cultural & Bookstore is a 501 (c) (3) nonprofit corporation funded
in part over the years by the National Endowment for the Arts, California Arts Council,
Los Angeles County Arts Commission, Los Angeles Department of Cultural Affairs, The
California Community Foundation, the Annenberg Foundation, the Weingart Founda-
tion, the Lia Fund, National Association of Latino Arts and Culture, Ford Foundation,
MetLife, Southwest Airlines, the Andy Warhol Foundation for the Visual Arts, the Thrill
Hill Foundation, the Middleton Foundation, Center for Cultural Innovation, John Irvine
Foundation, Not Just Us Foundation, the Attias Family Foundation, and the Guacamole
Fund, among others. Donations have also come from Bruce Springsteen, John Densmore
of The Doors, Jackson Browne, Lou Adler, Richard Foos, Gary Stewart, Charles Wright,
Adrienne Rich, Tom Hayden, Dave Marsh, Jack Kornfield, Jesus Trevino, David Sandoval,
Gary Soto, Denise Chávez and John Randall of the Border Book Festival, Luis & Trini
Rodríguez, and others.*

for
Dr. Noël Valis
who believed the girls could write
&
Dr. Diana Frade
who saved them so they could

Write as you will
In whatever style you like.
Too much blood has run under the bridge
To go on believing
That only one road is right.

In poetry everything is permitted
With only this condition, of course,

You have to improve the blank page.

— *Nicanor Parra*

Contents

FOREWORD

We Are Alive!

HERE IS A FOLDED PAPER slipped under the door. When you or I open the door—maybe only the sound of footsteps or a blur of brown curls descending the stairs—but in our hands the folded paper, and inside, the voice of a living girl. Oh, I was busy. I put off reading these poems—so busy, too many things to read, already late. You know the rest of the story: as soon as I started I couldn't stop. *Listen to this,* I kept saying to my daughter who was trying to finish her homework. Listen to this, I'd say out loud, laughing, or almost in tears.

Spencer Reece, poet and priest, spent a year in Honduras living in the orphanage itself behind the high wall that protected the girls from rape, trafficking, and murder. He taught poetry at the orphanage and in a nearby school. "Don't forget us," one girl, sitting alone on the stairs, said to Spencer on his last evening there. She is still there with the others, behind the high wall. But now these voices rise over the wall and reach us. They can be with us. And we can be with them.

Songs, odes, confessions and blessings, borrowing fairy tales, these poems reach out to us with the urgency of Keats' living hand. *We are alive!* The poems cry. We are behind the high wall. We are invisible to you, but we are here. The poems rise over the wall. Then they are with us, and we are with them.

—*Marie Howe*

INTRODUCTION

A Confession

Woman, why do you involve me?
—*John 2:4*

"Honey, we don't do no head transplants at Hartford Hospital," a nurse yells over her shoulder. Her name is Janice, her skin plum-black and her hair a braid circling and intricately pinned around her scalp. She smiles at me, bemused by the middle-aged white man alone in the inner-city that all the whites fled decades ago. I am rushing behind her, my first night as a chaplain. I am a seminarian doing my Clinical Pastoral Education. The ER has victims of gang violence, many of whom do not speak English. "Honey," she says, "The blacks shoot each other, the Puerto Ricans knife each other—it's more personal." A one-thousand bed Trauma 1 hospital, it has a helicopter called a Trauma Hawk that lands on the roof. The ER fills with blood jets, screams, as I fixate on a severed limb on a metal cart and Janice with a pair of scissors cutting off the clothes of the decapitated man before us.

...

One night in 2009 a boy and his mother enter Hartford Hospital. The boy has been stabbed in the chest twenty-five times, and the nurses page a chaplain named Father Spencer in his black clericals and white collar to attend. When I arrive I am told to aid the mother in her grief. The Puerto Rican mother does not speak English. At 6 AM the boy dies. After being up for thirty hours, I call my bishop, a Cuban American who navigates two languages, and I say to him that I have to learn Spanish, I cannot continue the song and dance with the black uniform and everyone calling me "Father." Without knowing Spanish, I feel a fraud.

The bishop says, "I have just the place for you."

I say, "Where's that?"

He says, "San Pedro Sula, Honduras. There is an orphanage for girls there. Get a grant and go in the summer and you will start learning Spanish."

I say, "Where's Honduras?"

"Central America," he says.

...

In 2010, I spend two months in that orphanage. Pretty much in silence. I don't feel like I'm contributing. Spanish frustrates me. I stand like a telephone pole in the middle of the courtyard with the screaming girls. All around my feet are decapitated Barbie doll heads. What on earth am I doing here? I don't categorize myself as a "kid person." Gay, with a long story of accepting that, I never consider working with children as anything close to what my ministry will entail: the idea of a gay man who is a priest working with children sounds like something I want to avoid—hospice sounds better. Granted they're girls and I'm gay which serves to cancel out the specter of a sex scandal, but, on the whole, children seem much harder to control than someone dying. The dying seem less threatening. I don't feel children calling me.

After two months of verbs and rain and lizards and electrical shortages, my bags are packed and I am ready to return to America. However, the poverty I see and smell and taste and feel and touch in one of the poorest Spanish-speaking countries in the western hemisphere is a part of me now: the beggars at the street corner, the sweet cheap perfume of the prostitutes, the grit, the beans and rice. What will I do with my witnessing? The love of the people is in me too: the way they accept me, hug me, are grateful for me. Me! An unlikely priest now in an unlikely place, every third moment in Honduras starts to surprise me. As someone with back-pew church attendance, the up-close, kissy affirmation of the girls, almost greedy, starts to change me. I don't quite notice this happening at first. A little girl wants to climb on top of my shoulders with soiled pants, another picks my nose, another braids my few hairs. But would they accept me fully if they knew more about me? For I never speak much about my life. But I am used to that. In the main, that seems appropriate with children. Especially, I think, these Honduran children with all their trauma do not need to know about me.

The last night I walk up to my apartment. A young girl named Gwendolyn waits for me outside my front door. I say, "What are you doing here?"

She says nothing. Silence. She looks up at the stars, looks over the twenty-foot wall. Someone burns plastic.

I say, "Is there something you want to tell me?" Gwendolyn pauses. There is that awkwardness that comes when two people speak in second languages.

She says, "Yes, Mister." For most of my time there they will call me Mister. I keep wondering if this is a left-over fragment from colonialism. They say it in a Spanish way, drawing out the vowel so the "i" is a long "e" sound, Miiiiister.

"I leave tomorrow," I say, surprised by my statement and wanting to keep the conversation going.

"We know," she says. We. She speaks for all of them? Like a messenger from the Bible? That they know I'm leaving surprises me because I don't think any child there has tracked my deaf mute existence.

"What is it you want to tell me?" I ask. Another pause.

The palm fronds blow in the night breeze. Then Gwendolyn says, "Don't forget us."

I pause. Haltingly, like an actor unsure of my lines, I say, "No, no, of course, I won't forget you." It sounds awkward in my mouth as I wonder how many times she has heard that. Something is happening in slow motion. I generally hunger for authenticity, and I deplore saying what I don't mean. Do I mean it? I want to mean it. I close the door behind me. Look at my luggage. The girls' faces flood my head. I'm jittery from her plea and her look that has somehow pierced me. They need advocates, clear for anyone to see. But me? Seriously? How can I—white, male, Midwestern—honor her? Why not someone closer to her experience? A Latina poet for example? Why not someone more politically engaged? I am no Adrienne Rich. My understanding of social justice is thin. Why not, for that matter, someone who speaks better Spanish? Maybe Gwendolyn says it to every gringo who passes through here?

Despite all the negative doubts clouding my brain I start to wonder, How can I honor this request? Maybe—I think quickly—the way I do when in the middle of writing a poem—poetry can respond creatively to this plea. Curiously, I don't think religiously in this moment. The word "anthology" crosses my mind. The word "bilingual" enters my brain. But I've never taught and I am new to translation and I've never done an anthology. And why am I standing in the middle of the room crying? Perhaps it is because without realizing it I am saying, "Yes." Against all odds. On paper, this isn't looking good.

Yes, Gwendolyn, yes.

I've felt many things in my life, but never, growing up in the States, have I ever worried as a child that I would be completely forgotten. If anything, I'd been over-monitored. Once I got on the wrong school bus at six and my mother practically had a nervous breakdown when I didn't show up at home. A child feeling like they would be forgotten. Shouldn't be. Shouldn't be like that, I say to the bare room with my packed luggage.

Subtly, unwittingly, Gwendolyn's plea starts to push me onto my road to Damascus, it is this plea that will knock me off my horse and open me utterly to God's love. When I go back to

Yale for my final year in seminary, people say to me, "You're different." The assessment comes unprompted and often. I can't stop talking about the girls. I squeeze them into every dry theological conversation: I become obsessed. About to have that collar around my neck I begin to think such a collar might encircle something with the girls.

I apply for a Fulbright in 2012 after seminary and I am rejected in the final round. I apply again in 2013 and I am accepted. With the aid of a Fulbright grant for poetry (no funding from a church), I live in Honduras for one year as a priest and teacher. I put together this anthology to honor Gwendolyn's request and invite a film crew to make a documentary film about the girls. I'm a brand new priest. I'm unsteady in that role although not unsure of the choice. Poetry is what I know most and best. But I'm also realistic: poetry book sales barely break even in publishing houses. A well-known publisher of poetry said to me that waiting on poetry sales was like throwing a rose petal into the Grand Canyon and waiting for the echo. A film might reach more.

...

Honduras is the second largest country in Central America, after Nicaragua. Shaped almost like Texas, Honduras looks like an angel with its arms outstretched and its head missing. There are eight million Hondurans but one million live outside the country. This absent million mainly work in the United States illegally, sending their money back home. In recent years, drug gangs from Mexico have moved in. Violence and drug trafficking has increased. Planes filled with cocaine fly over the one story cinder-block houses in faded pastel colors. The banana industry, once the foundation of the economy, has declined from global competition. Hurricane Mitch, in 1998, blighted many plantations. The year I live there, 24,000 Honduran children without parents are found on the United States border trying to enter, either to find work or to find their parents; and within

Honduras, one thousand young people under the age of twenty-three are killed. The year I go, the number of children at the border doubles. Within the span of one month, 32 children are killed, one under the age of two. One girl, from Mexico, after being sent back twice, at the age of fourteen, will hang herself in a US detention center. In San Pedro Sula, the sound of the rain on the tin roofs mixes with the sound of the bare feet of children fleeing the city.

Honduras is a country of two hundred thousand orphans. Our Little Roses, where I live and work for a year from Christmas to Christmas, is the only all-girl orphanage in the country. Girls, much discounted in Honduran culture before the founding of this home, were sent to the women's state penitentiary for the inmates to look after them. A judge, opposed to the founding of the home, had said to the founder: "If you open this home where will we get our maids and prostitutes?" What's more, the judge was a woman. Misogyny ingrained exactly as homophobia had been ingrained in me. A shudder goes through me as I hear this story. I don't quite understand it and I won't for a long time, but something strange and eerie is happening as I recognize and understand things related to these girls who seem so utterly different from me.

Adoption has been discouraged for years in Honduras because the government found too many adopted children showing up in the sex trade in the United States. The idea of Our Little Roses was to raise the girls in the country. The goal was not to abandon Honduras. It's been a challenge.

...

My apartment is in the same building as the school where I teach, on the same grounds as the orphanage. My apartment is one of the few places with air-conditioning. The sound of it muffles the world outside: the birds, the taxis, the dirty donkeys with their drivers collecting trash, the children. However, the chapel is directly beneath me. And when services start going every morning with the electric piano, the whole place shakes with a wild colorful Central American joy: as if Christ is coming down to earth on an ice cream truck at 7 AM. I will learn whimsy is the most common response in Honduras to the direst of circumstances.

Come closer. Let me show you the place. There's a big metal gate at the entrance to the street that clangs and rolls back on wheels. There's a square brick building with a clay tiled roof that houses 72 girls in a preponderance of bunk beds. There's a lunchroom, library, and a central courtyard with a fountain where a small turtle is often tortured. Behind this is a two-story structure that houses the school and my apartment. Behind that is a tin-roofed cancha with a cement floor and bleachers for endless soccer games. The girls' tough foot-soles sliding across the cement as they play sounds like a person rapidly flipping pages of a book. At the back of that is a two-story cement wall painted with a giant colorful mural. Behind that, a tight little triangle of land, a hiding place with a mango tree where the girls do secret things. The whole place is surrounded by a high wall and garlanded with barbed-wire and protected by twenty-four hour round-the-clock armed guards. Often young boys climb the walls and whistle at the girls through the wire, saying "*Carne fresca!*" "Fresh meat." It's less prison. More oasis.

...

I teach in the co-ed bilingual school. The school caters to children from the neighborhood. Girls from the home are mixed into the student population, about 10 percent of the 200 students. I teach English as a second language with the specific aim of teaching poetry, memorizing it and writing it, something that has never been done before in this place. I specifically want to draw out what those girls have to say. That ten percent. The ones that never leave the grounds when the others go out the metal gate and home to families. I'm following Gwendolyn's direction. Curious to note, once I get there Gwendolyn rarely speaks to me. She seems to be saying, "I've done my part, now get to work."

My class all year starts at 7:30 AM. The bell goes off. A stampede of teenage girls and boys. I stand at the front of the classroom. The students whisper things in Spanish impossibly fast for my newly accustomed ears. Despite all the cognates, Spanish is quite different from English and my Spanish is weak. I have just come from a year in Spain where I took four hours of language classes five days a week for nine months. I have a strange elegant lisp. The girls look at me like I'm a circus freak.

Each night after a day of teaching, I sit at a long wooden table for dinner with twenty little girls poised to tease me relentlessly; usually their game consists of asking me who's my girlfriend. When I point to one of them and say, "This one," that one rejects me immediately with mock disdain. They say, *Que asco!* which means Yuck! They all laugh. Mightily. Call me *chancho* which means pig. This game goes on for the entire year as the upper grade girls write their poems.

Around this time, Leyli, age 16, writes in her diary. It will be her only diary entry:

> *On Thursday the psychologist gave me some medicine for my depression and he told me that when I started to drink the medicine I will not eat a lot of food. That day Patsy's group was here and we played and made some cards for our friends in Nashville. That day after making some of the cards we made some cookies and we had to give some to a friend. I gave some of my cookies to Suyapita because she was telling me that she wanted more cookies. So I gave her the cookies. On Saturday we made more cards for more friends and I met with Mister Spencer to work on my poem and I did not want to work because I was tired and I wanted to sleep and because I wanted to read another book and because I don't like to write poems because it is boring. On Saturday night I started to read a new book, a very good book, called* Bitterblue. *On Sunday we*

went to church here at the chapel and Mister Spencer read my poem. After church we went to the movies and we saw Monster Inc. *in 3D and after the movie we made a drama about the stories of Jesus.*

...

For much of my time there I'll keep thinking I am the last person on earth for this work. I will often imagine a Latina lesbian embracing the work with gusto and insight, but this mythical lesbian never shows up. I think I could have that "better suited person" on the front line teaching and I, with my Fulbright, could be in the back, taking notes, detached, safe, in the background. I could be an observer! Actually, a Latina lesbian does show up early on but it doesn't work out. I invite her to co-teach some of the classes but she weirdly doesn't take to the work. I make other attempts to hand over the work, but each time it doesn't quite work and I find myself center stage once more. Despite every attempt to hand over this project to someone I think more appropriate, that imagined person, whatever I imagine, never appears for long, and so by default, it falls squarely and unequivocally on me.

The classes don't go well for many weeks. I'm awkward. Respect for me seems nil. There's a girl who sleeps through the entire class every week. When I stand next to the white board, my pens frequently never work. School supplies are scarce. The copy machine never works. Some days we have no water. Some no electricity. Some days we have no class, a mysterious string of fiestas that seem especially designed to interrupt my ability to teach. Living that close to the equator, the tyranny of heat debilitates. Girls from the orphanage have deep issues of abandonment; they can be moody, and I am no trained psychologist. Many of them are hitting puberty and what do I know about menstruation? They live in dormitories where lights go on and off all night like in a hospital, compromising their concentration. And lest I forget, they have no parents. In strange flitting moments, seeing Ana Ruth with her pencil case and books, I realize with brute force that I had parents. Perhaps that seems like a simple and obvious thought, but at times I forget the simple and obvious. Granted, I had suffered a great estrangement from my parents over my sexuality. Ten years went by without speaking. I had judged them harshly for their part. Now I feel regret. I experience unexpected gratefulness towards my parents. Honduras affects me that way. Those girls. While gratitude for my parents increases, and compassion for the lives of the girls expands, my anxiety also mounts because I am beginning to wonder if any poetry is ever going to get written under these circumstances. Maybe this idea of mine is ill-conceived. I'm quite certain many are saying as much behind my back.

...

I forge ahead with little progress. Somehow I cannot and will not let Gwendolyn down. As I teach, the American documentary film crew starts production. They end up coming four separate times: in the beginning, in the middle, in the end, and after I am gone. There are four of them on the ground with me, three in their twenties: Carmen Delaney, the cinematographer, bright red-hair, a nose ring, exacting yet cheerful; Cassidy Friedman, secondary cinematographer, affable and quick-witted, thin handsome soccer body, who the girls fixate on with their crushes; Kevin Oliver, tall, thin, shy, gay, does sound and understands my silences about girlfriends. And then there's Brad Coley, the director, closer to my age, his hair standing up like Einstein most days, Ivy League educated, years of film-making in New York—dedicated, passionate, his brown eyes always widening as he attempts to consider how to hold all of this complicated story together. As we move in a pack across the compound I think this might be what it was like to be with the disciples moving with their nets along the shore after Jesus. Others are involved behind the scenes, such as Elise Durant, a woman who edited for Woody Allen and who will shrink 250 hours of footage down to an hour and twenty minutes.

The crew spends their days focused on the girls. The crew can clearly see how difficult the girls are being, but this does not seem to concern them. Perhaps it will be a film of girls being difficult? And a documentary of my abysmal failure? I don't like the sound of that but too much has now been set in motion to turn back. A part of me (I think I will now call it faith) stubbornly believes these girls can write poems.

At times, after another day of disastrous teaching, the focus turns to me. The crew or the girls want to know more of my biography. To Brad I say, "The girls don't need to know about me. I am better kept in the background." Brad does not say anything in these attempts of mine to deflect and keeps filming the girls. This starts to feel ominous to me. At the same time, the girls begin to ask me more questions. Where did I grow up? Was I in love? What is my story? My resistance to talking about myself matches, if not surpasses, the girls resistance to writing about themselves.

...

As my teaching seems to get worse something begins to gnaw at me. Honduras has been a land decimated by imperial forces: the Spaniards, the British, the North Americans. Each made the "banana republic" more flimsy, handing it down to the next invader, pillaging it for what they wanted or needed, exploiting the locals and leaving. I begin to feel I cannot be one more gringo with good intentions, asking the girls to bare their souls in their poems and not bare my own. Yet I'm not so comfortable with the idea of baring my soul. I justify my need to remain aloof: the girls do not need to know about their teacher having suicide attempts, a period of being locked-up in a loony bin, estranged for a decade from family, and having come out of the closet late in life with questionably few successful romances to his name. They most certainly do not need to know that, right?

...

One minute the girls stretch out over the film crew like cats and the next minute they are frightened tensed animals in a petting zoo. Missionary groups come and go, numbing them to abandonment. They know how to present a front. So do I. Having grown up in Minnesota in the 1970s I needed to hide my gayness in order to survive, hide it as best I could. And of course another part of the story is I´d had several girlfriends I´d loved as best I could through my twenties and thirties, so I was not immune to the charms of the fairer sex. Under the many layers of my psychological varnish, I can play the girls' game of camouflage, and in addition I have fifty or so years on them. Sometimes I think they are looking at me as quizzically as I am looking at them. What mysteries we all are.

I hear the desolate horrible silence after all the guests leave. I feel the collective sigh of the girls like a soft wind through the home when we are together with the armed guards and each other, and everyone has left, left us with presents, good wishes, but in the end, left us. I smell the soiled diapers. I turn to one of the girls, Jasmin, and say: "How do you deal with this silence, after all the guests go?"

"Oh," she says in Spanish, with a drained expression, "You will get used to it, and besides…" Here she pauses, looks over the courtyard, some of the girls having retreated to their bunk beds, exhausted, and says, "We have each other."

One day I leave for a week and say to one of the girls, Patricia, that I will be back in one week. She nods her head. When I go back the following week I see her. She is in a school uniform impossibly big for her, white shirt with blue skirt. Her backpack heavy. When she sees me she looks at the ground. I hug her. She will not let go of me. I think it's the heat, our unending heat— sometimes it feels like we are frying. She cries, but not like a sobbing child—her crying is interior, circumspect, evolved.

I say, "You, Patricia, you're my girlfriend; *Vos, Patricia, vos eres mi novia*." She nods and does not reject me. No calling me *chancho* this time. She just leans into me in that too-big uniform in the middle of the dusty street with donkeys and carts and taxis with tinted windows.

...

About two months into my time there, I am completely exasperated. The girls do not want to write poems. They are not paying attention. I begin to doubt this whole endeavor and call the founder in the States. She says, "I'm coming down from Miami soon. Wait until I get there. There are things you don't know."

Dr. Diana Frade (pronounced like Friday), founded the home twenty-five years ago. The government gave her five acres next to the worst barrio in the city. And from that place all this has sprung. She got Desmond Tutu to place one of the first shovels in the ground. She has her own hardscrabble story: a young woman from Kansas, she'd fallen in love with a Latino man, who never really gets named no matter how many times I hear her tell this story, and the unnamed man brought her to Honduras many years ago where they married, had two boys, and then he left her. Here's where the story takes an unusual twist: she stayed. Raised her boys alone and ran a dress store. Of those years she once said to me, looking away, "They were lonely years. Very lonely."

Later in life, she married my bishop from Miami and opened this home. Tall and blond with blue eyes that pierce her face like stars, she stands out in a country of short cocoa-skinned people. She's able to solve problems in seconds when faced with power outages or undisciplined girls. She's lived in Honduras forty years and feels more Honduran than American. "I saw a picture of myself the other day with several Honduran women and I was shocked by the blonde woman in the center of the photograph. It was me! I'd lived here so long I'd forgotten I looked so different. I love this country." She speaks wistfully and says, "I can't believe what has happened here—it wasn't always like this. It makes me sad for my country." The headlines about corruption, coups and murders make her heart sink. How she keeps popping up behind her metal desk in her office again and again with indefatigable optimism astonishes me.

I go to her office down the hallway. All my keys on a string clang around my neck. I look grim as a jailer. The kids laugh and yell in their uniforms. I believe they are mainly laughing at me. It's a lonely business. I push through the glass door to her office. We eat bananas and have another cup of coffee, just picked from the plantation, which often works in Honduras like a truth serum.

She says, "You see that girl in your 11th grade class? The one that has been giving you trouble. Let me tell you about her. At the age of four her mother gave her away to a stepmother. The stepmother tied a rock around her neck and threw her in a well. She screamed for days. A neighbor found her and brought her to our doorstep. She's been here for fourteen years and no one has ever come to visit her on Family Day. This home is all she's got. This is it." Frade turns her head then, tears in her eyes, and looks out the window at the world she has built, two hundred kids laughing with a lightness in their step, bouncing balls, eating *baleadas*. In the softest voice, almost a whisper, she says of the girl, recalling the day she arrived at the home at age four, "She was so little. So little."

...

Out the classroom window are the mountains, blue on blue on blue, and mangoes hang from their delicate stems, ripe and orange. There is the girl, smiling shyly, holding her pencil, her uniform pressed, waiting for me in my classroom. If she writes a poem, I think, wonderful. If not, fine. With that one singular story from the founder, the image of the girl trapped in the well emblazoned in my mind, my teaching changes. The girl and I sit in the courtyard after class. The turtle twitches. I give the girl one prompt. I say, "Use the word charity." What comes back is her truth:

What is home for you?
Your school can be your home
even if you don't have a bed.
Living here has been like
tasting cotton candy:
it is that sweet.

The poem changes me the minute I see it, hear it, digest it. I awaken. The next day I come up with new bizarre methods for teaching. The textbooks from Texas with ripped pages that have been handed down year after year seem to kill the energy, so I ask the girls to drop them, heavy as gravestones on the floor, never to be picked up again. The eyes of the girls widen. There's a little mischief now in that room. And perhaps they pick up a whiff of what has gone down with me in the founder's office. Somehow there's more love in me for them than before because of that story. And somehow I think the girls can smell it.

I say to them, "Look at me! *Mírame!*" I radically decide to pare down the teaching. All I deploy is spoken words in the air. "Listen to this," I say and I begin to recite. They fidget just a little less—and do I see out of the corner of my eye that sleeping girl shift her head just a little? Has she really been listening the entire time? Waiting for me to do something sincere? "Now you say it," I say. The girls tighten up a bit. "That's right, take out your pencils and write down what I am saying, I will say it again." They do it. And that's when the world opens up a little bit between them and me.

What works is me saying the poems to them. What works is them saying the poems back. What works is a sort of call and response. What works is them memorizing the poems. We harken back to poetry's oral tradition. This way, the poetry feels invisible. Like those girls. Like Honduras. Like, for so much of my own life, me.

I have memorized about twenty poems. So those are the ones I deploy. We start with William Shakespeare's Sonnet 18:

"Shall I compare thee to a summer's day," it begins. I say, "Okay, here's the poem. I'll say it and you'll write down what you hear. If you don't have paper then come to the blackboard. Then I'll say it again. *¿Me explico?* Then you'll memorize it too. *¿Entiendes?* Then you'll write it down from memory. We'll have vocabulary quizzes on each word you do not know. That's it. *Nada más.* One poem per semester. *Es lo que hay.* No textbooks. No paper. And you'll keep a diary. I don't care what you write, just something. And after school we'll meet and write your own first poems together." So it begins. Me and them.

What's more, the girls need to move. I need to move. They look awkwardly straightjacketed in their navy blue school uniforms. We are always sweating. Our foreheads look like windows after a rainstorm within seconds. The following week I find a pitifully old boom-box and a recording of Diana Ross and The Supremes singing "Stop in the Name of Love." I say, "After every vocabulary quiz we dance to The Supremes. For twenty minutes." When I tell them this at first they look at me stunned as if to say, "You've got to be kidding me, Mister." But it doesn't take long to convince them. There we go, the girls fluid and undulating, and me, the old gringo busting a move.

...

The year wears on: nights with gunshots and mornings with black metallic birds cawing, white steeples overlooking the barrio where a small child with a bloated stomach moves in and out of a cardboard box and desperate mothers crawl over the dump searching for food scraps. Tennis shoes tied to electrical wires indicate where one gang's territory ends and another begins. In the orphanage, a gentle laughter amongst the girls and the women who look after them.

Students memorize Jane Kenyon's "Let Evening Come," W.H. Auden's "The More Loving One," Emily Dickinson's "I'm Nobody! Who Are You?" Elizabeth Bishop's "One Art," William Blake's "Jerusalem," an anonymous poem from the Terezin concentration camp, and the twenty-third psalm, King James version. An eclectic selection I realize, but it is simply what is in my head and that'll have to suffice with an Internet that goes out every rain storm. While they memorize, I witness their faces—their cheeks lift into joyfulness, their eyes focus on a materializing horizon like a horde of explorers.

Roberto Sosa, a well-known Honduran poet who died the year before I arrive, said, "It is practically a poetic country. There are more poets than almost anywhere." Our classroom starts to prove that boast. Local Honduran poets visit. The girls grow articulate and more confident. Poetry is not beyond them. The poems not only come out of their hands but memorized poems pour out of their mouths. One after another the girls recite and recite and recite. They recite Shakespeare for the board members. Not a dry eye among the businessmen and attorneys.

The girls write poems first in Spanish, then translate them into English, or first in English and then in Spanish. Girls are protective of their stories. Some are truculent, intractable, mercurial, stubborn. I realize their personal stories and the beds they sleep in are what they have, very often, all they have, so exposing that to strangers does not happen quickly, and sometimes it feels like it will never happen, and that, too, becomes fine with me. Exposing feelings is delicate surgery. They get grumpy and snappy like the turtle they torture in the courtyard. One girl writes, "It is horrible to know you've been thrown away." I think, "Careful, Spencer." Some of the girls will only publish anonymously—like Dickinson before them, the idea of publication horrifies them. It's like "publishing your soul," Dickinson had said. And yet in the same breath many of them also want to be known. Dickinson sent 575 of her poems out in letters. So a part of her wanted to be heard. This contradiction of being heard and not seen, this treading on very vulnerable ground in poetry, is something I intuitively understand. Often in my own writing life I have felt a push and a pull between recognition and anonymity, and I think many a poet has felt or will feel the same. The soul needs protecting.

I start inventing assignments. The first assignment comes out of nativity figurines I find in the trash. These clay figures are called *adornos*. Each child picks one and writes in the voice of what she picks. One picks a cathedral, another picks a donkey, and yet another picks a headless woman. The poem in this collection, "A Honduran Story," comes from Katherine staring at a clay wedded couple and imagining what they might say. The next semester I change tack and I ask the older children to write stories to the younger children. The girls only know one popular fairy tale called *La Llorona* which centers on an ugly deranged woman who kills her children and throws them in a ditch, so it seems there's room for improvement. The girls invent new fairy tales with Honduran twists: Honduras and the five dwarves attacked by a witch represented by Spain; Ana Ruth's Red Riding Hood becomes "Little Red Hot Lips," and Ana Cecelia, her twin sister, writes a modern "Beauty & the Beast."

...

On Mother's Day Ana Cecelia, whose mother died of cirrhosis, hepatitis, and poverty, writes in her diary:

> *I don't like poetry. But I enjoy the Literature class with Mr. Spencer anyway. The best part is when we spend time with the little kids. They talk about what they want to have in our "fable poems." It surprised me to see how the little kids would open their minds and start imagining things. Today at the school we celebrated Mother's Day. I watched the celebration and it was not bad at all. I noticed that the mothers who belong to the kids from the neighborhood were enjoying the program. It ended early. I felt nothing.*

...

Loss looms large in our classroom, large as the blue mountains out the window. No amount of Christmas presents or sponsors in the States or gringos dressed up as Easter bunnies seems to cancel it out. Now you might think, as a result, everything I receive from the girls would be sad. But this is where things become more illuminated for me, more strange and intriguing. Nine times out of ten the poems come back with joy and forgiveness and hope. Leyli, beaten senseless by her mother, writes:

> When I was six I saw my parents a few times, between one and four in the afternoon. I forgot their names. When I look up at the sky I do not wonder about them. I am going to play and I am going to dance to have some fun with the dark shadows. I will be a happy girl.

To the greatest horror, Leyli responds with whimsy. This begins to feel to me quintessentially Honduran: next to the world's worst barrio a mural of a triumphant girl painted in electric hot pink and lime green and bright yellow.

...

Students have trouble with meter. After all, Spanish is accented differently and English rhythm is subtler. I want them to understand meter in Auden and Dickinson. One day trying to figure this out, I hear the sounds of salsa coming through my window. I ask my students how many beats are in salsa. Four, they say, usually, looking at me with teenage disdain for my adult gringo ignorance. I say, "Perfect." So it comes to pass, in chapel, my students dance and recite Dickinson's "I'm Nobody! Who are you?" with me in the background pressing down the salsa beat button on the electric piano. There is Dickinson, presented full blast with explosive hip thrusts, before the school assembly that sits mystified in church pews.

...

Tick tock—my last days approach, along with mounting enthusiasm for poetry. We plaster the school hallways with poems. One girl, who is not in any of my classes and speaks no English, hands me a piece of paper crumpled into a ball, and says, "For you, Mister." It will be the poem, "Invisible for All My Life." Another day a girl from the home comes to me—one who had been stabbing her pencil into the sofa when we met privately and saying that poetry was boring. Now she comes to me and says, shoulder back, "Yes, Mister, I want to recite the Langston Hughes poem about Helen Keller." When she does, she does so with more confidence than I've seen before. Where did it come from? For months she has not wanted any attention paid to her for being an orphan, has emphatically stated she wants her poem to be anonymous. After the Hughes recitation, she comes to my desk, looks out the window and says, "Hey Mister, I want my name in the book." Gently, I tap the letters of her name onto the keyboard, and save the name into the document, a name she says she's hated most of her life: Leyli Karolina Figueroa Rodríguez.

...

And then there's Aylin. She sometimes gets good grades, other times she flunks. The year she's my student, she´s on academic probation. She has grown up in the home from a young age and her English is strong from all the contact she has had from missionaries. Moving her pretty body in a street hip-hop way, her voice is surprisingly deep and husky. She's difficult: she entices the film crew then shuts them out, toying with them. The story I get of Aylin is that her mother said to Aylin and her three sisters that she was taking them on a trip to visit the orphan girls at Our Little Roses. The mother had framed it as an outing of charity. But the mother abandoned the girls there. The mother walked out the front gate with her only son and a new boyfriend and went to Mexico, the Latino macho culture's prizing of the male child hideously on display in this story. Aylin wailed. In ten years the mother never has been to visit Aylin. As far as I know Aylin rarely hears from her. From what I see, the child abandoned by a parent who is alive is far different from the child whose parents are dead. The self-esteem of the abandoned child with a living parent is a harder thing to recast.

I often work on the poems with the students in after school sessions. My teaching seems to be improving and this is my third and final full semester with the girls. Aylin is not impressed, rarely looks at me, and has no interest in private sessions. Sometimes I border collie the students to get them to write, prompting in Spanish, prompting in English, to use an adjective here or a metaphor there. But not Aylin.

That semester she memorizes the twenty-third psalm, King James version, ending:

> *Surely goodness and mercy shall follow me all the days of my life:*
> *And I will dwell in the house of the LORD for ever.*

I have continual discipline problems with her. Finally we go to the principal's office together because one day after school a small rock gets thrown at my head and she is behind me and laughs, mocking me. I grab her by the arm and she bucks like a wild colt (I believe I even said something my mother might have said, "Now listen here young lady!"). Certainly it could have been a rock hurled by one of the gangs who perch on the tops of the walls. That happens now and again. Or it could have been Aylin. Still, her disrespect and laughter irritates me. A tía comforts me and says it isn't a rock, just a hard seed that feels like a rock which is well-meaning enough but it still felt like a rock, and rock or seed, it was Aylin's attitude that was in question. Little is accomplished in the principal's office and the result is that Aylin gives me the silent treatment for a few months, which one notices when one lives in a compound.

Now I could dismiss her, carry my own grudge against her

insolence. It would be easy enough for me to ignore this girl. And I have my own history of grudges I am ashamed to admit. But at this moment when Aylin and I cross paths, I have a growing awareness that resentment and more silent treatments are not the answers I am seeking.

In the Gospel of Mark there appears the story of Herod and his wife and John the Baptist. Herod's wife carries a grudge and eventually asks for the head of John the Baptist on a silver platter. She gets what she wants and that's the end of John the Baptist. The grudge kills him. No more beautiful words from that evangelist. I'd done much the same as Herod's wife, eliminating people from my life if they annoyed me enough or didn't behave the way I wanted them to behave, sentencing them to permanent silence in my world. But I was tired of that narrative. And so I stayed open to difficult, troubled, smart, vexed Aylin.

Packing my suitcases, emailing the Bishop of Spain in Madrid who had just offered me a job (so my Spanish would continue!), in the flurry of starting my adioses, Aylin hands in her poem. The poem is called, "Counting." She's folded it into squares and she hands it over to me, not really looking at me, and says, "Here it is Mister, don't change a word." The students flee the classroom and I open the piece of paper and it won't be the first time their poems startle me. It's a prose poem which I had talked to them about, a way to get them out of the box of thinking about meter or rhyme.

The final assignment I'd made up was to write a poem to a person who was no longer in Honduras, someone who'd left. On the first day of class I asked them to raise their hand if they knew someone who had left their country. Every child raised her hand. "So that's what we ´ll write about," I said. And as an after-thought, for some reason, and I don't know why, I said, "They'll be prayers. Prayer poems." Aylin's is written to God about her mother. Every other kid writes a poem to an actual someone, but Aylin's is the only one directly to God:

> *It is ugly to know that everyone in this school is celebrating Mother's Day. On this day, I feel ashamed to be me.*

But, God, listen to this: I am counting time like people count stars and I will keep counting until my mother comes. My sisters are graduating and soon I will go to college too. When I graduate from college and when I am finally somebody in this world, God, I will go straight to Mexico where my mother lives and I will stare at her like I stare at the stars and with a voice that cracks like thunder I will say: I FORGIVE YOU! But for now, God, I am here, in Our Little Roses, counting.

There I stood, the kids running out to catch a bus or return to their bunk beds. If Herod's wife had not ordered the decapitation of John imagine what messages he might have had for this world, what more he might have said. Grudges and resentments shrink the world, and acceptance and forgiveness expand it. Those girls, what they teach me. The poem stuns me with its acceptance and forgiveness, it is not what I expected. I too speak to God in that moment in my empty classroom and am grateful I chose to stay open to Aylin so I too could be taught a thing or two.

...

Ismelda, age 16, is in my final class, along with Aylin. Her mother is dead and her father hardly ever comes to visit. She has glasses and sits attentively in the front row with her notebook every day. She likes to dance. Sometimes she seems far away, like she isn't paying any attention to what I am saying, as I stand at the front of the class with my *guayabera* white priest shirt, my foul coffee breath, gesticulating madly about poems before we start to do the dance routine from the musical Grease, shimmying like John Travolta and Olivia Newton John (it wasn't my favorite, but my selections were limited). I can't tell if anything I am saying is making any kind of impression on her. I worry about this. One day in her diary, she writes:

First of all, I just want to say that I am happy to be in this school and this home. Our Little Roses, 'cause a lot was bad for me when I didn't live here. My life was so bad. And now that I am here in this bilingual school I have lots of friends. I never dreamed I would have so many friends like I have now; I didn't know these friends would change my life 'cause when I was little I didn't have this place. The friends I had outside of this place were always hitting me, throwing rocks at me and in that time I thought my life was a disaster. It was difficult for me to have friends. But as you can see God is good. Don´t forget that, Mister Spencer. God is always going to be with you. It doesn't matter if you don't see him 'cause he is always in our heart in the bad things and in the good things. Don't forget, Mister Spencer, that your life can change in any moment with the presence of God. Mister Spencer, I always have that, and I want you to know that my life has changed.

Those girls. Teaching me when all the time I am so worried about what I am teaching them.

...

Under the *cancha's* tin corrugated canopy, we have our *Espectáculo*, sharing our poems with the town. That night, exhausted, we doubt if we can pull this thing off. Although we've practiced every night after dinner for months, there have been horrible rehearsals. Once again I can't tell how to read the girls; they seem lethargic—do they want to do this? Sometimes I've noticed a push/pull nuance between me and them: they are grateful and disdainful at the same time. We practice and practice our dance routines, the recitations, the miracle play, cueing the lights (well, one, we have one spotlight), the music, and the girls are unruly and *vagas*, meaning lazy. But, then, a kind of Honduran miracle: a river of townspeople stream in under the bright Central American moon and the girls start reciting and singing and standing proud in all their costumes the 2nd grade teacher made. There must be 200 people there. I am shocked. The girls shine and nary a mistake is made: the words are made flesh and the crowd is captivated. Jane Kenyon's poem can be heard on a video loop as girl after girl says, "Let evening come as it will and don't be afraid, God does not leave us comfortless." No one throws rocks over the wall that night. More poets than almost anywhere. Hadn't Sosa said that?

During the miracle play, I am humbled to a new level by a language gaffe, even for me! When one learns a new language at the age of 46 there seems to be no bottom to the humility, so much so that humility and humiliation become challenging to distinguish from each other at times. Standing before the parents and Diana Frade and an ambassador from the American embassy, I speak into the microphone narrating the play called, "Honduras and the Five Dwarves." At a certain point all the little children need to fall down, which requires a command from me, which should be ¡Cáiganse! But if you change two letters in cáiganse you get cáguense, drop the "i" and change an "a" for an "ue." ¡Cáguense! is an unusual command that translates as "Shit yourselves!" Standing before them, dressed in my priest uniform, guess which letters come up? Laughter is followed by shock and then a crowd of little mischievous smiles gathers around me like fireflies—that sense of whimsy again.

As the people leave, in big joyful groups, I see Aylin, who won the prize that night for her poem (we had a contest and placed the winning poet in a chair, a poet's chair the girls carved, creating a tradition to name a poet there every year). I say to her, and I don't know where it comes from, quite forcefully, "I love you!" Soren Kierkegaard, a Christian existentialist, says you need love to build love. Love has been building in me all year. I definitely do not want to romanticize this. Love often makes a mess. It certainly had done so within my own family. There follows with Aylin an awkward pause and then Aylin says, "I love you, too." No hug follows, or a smile, just that husky tom boy voice hanging in the air under the tin roof. She steps back, soccer ball under her arm and off, off, she goes into the night, hugged by the girls, back to her dormitory. Aylin.

...

I find my refuge in roses, in words.
— *Clarice Lispector*

On my second to last day, Brad, the film director, comes to me with his bird's nest of hair and asks me one last time to finally share my story with the girls before I leave. I immediately resist.

"I feel too vulnerable," I say, looking away, distracted. It is very hot and we are both sweating.

"But they are asking to know more about you," Brad says. I can hear Cassidy and Carmen talking nearby. If you had closed your eyes you might have thought he was speaking to one of the girls.

"I just don't want to do it," I say, surprised by my resistance. Alone, I go back to my apartment with the AC droning, it's like living inside an airplane, the way it sounds when you are in mid-air. I get down on my knees because I feel so off. Maybe it is the heat? But, then, I get the sinking feeling that maybe it is me. Sometimes being a priest can be a solitary thing, can feel lonely; teaching them I often felt alone, yet with them. And because peers are scarce I have no one to bounce off my insecurity. This gets me agitated. And just being an adult among teenagers working in a language that has so many holes in it for me, I often react to things emotionally at a much lower maturity level than I would in English. So, in short, I have doubts about how I had been with Brad.

But what had Ismelda written to me? God is always with me. Isn't that what she wrote? Something is off in me, I felt it when I spoke to Brad. It might very well be time to do the thing I don't want to do: share some of my story with the girls.

I leave my praying for a moment and go to the little laptop and click on Skype. I call Mary Jane Zapp, old friend and the photographer for this book, whose sensible counsel I´ve often sought over the years, and I explain my nervous awkward state. We look at each other through the tiny fragile window of the laptop that is working for the moment.

She says, "Why not just tell your story to *one* of the girls."

Now that is something I think I can do. How important this conferring, talking we do with one another, and in particular, how important it can be between a woman and a man, for women have insights men often don´t and particularly regarding the delicate surgery of emotions. We say good-bye. No time to dawdle. I click off from Skype. I go back to kneeling beside my bed. I start to pray again. I think: I can share my story, all of it, with one of the girls for the film, not a public declaration for the whole school, but an exchange of two, like a communion service, the way Jesus spoke to people—that, I think, kneeling there, AC droning, I can do, I can do that, no, I need to do that. Suddenly everything feels urgent.

I step over my packed luggage, the film crew following me, all of us sweating in the sauna of a Honduran twilight, I feel like I am back in the ER at Hartford Hospital, dizzy, out of place, yet in the exact right place, and in my final night I go to that girl, the one lodged permanently in my mind since I sat down with Diana Frade, the one who never wants her name on her poem in this anthology, the girl who has the home's most unspeakable story—found in a well with a rock around her neck—and I ask her this: "Would you listen to my story? For the film crew to hear?"

She says, "Ah, Mister, you know I don't want to be filmed, I hate the cameras…"

"No," I say, "This is about me being filmed, you just have to listen…" How foreign and right it suddenly feels that the focus turns on me. Although I'm not comfortable.

"Alright," she says, "But why me? You know I hate those cameras, Mister Spencer." And, indeed, I know she is repelled by them as much as she doesn´t like putting her name on her poem and about as much as I feel awkward with what I am about to do.

"I know, I know, but they will be filming me this time," I say.

The sky purples and the insects swarm the security lights. The film crew huddles around us. I pause. Then I start. I tell her before the cameras of those things that had kept me from church. And I do say church. That gets her attention. God and church and priests have a different level of respect in Honduras: priests are not jokes and God is not seen through an ironic lens as God most often is in the US or Europe. God is a real thing. She begins to pay more attention, I think, than when she was in class.

Out tumble my secrets, all of them—feeling always the loner, the outsider, odd, suicidal at times, locked up in a mental ward, unloved, different, estranged from family for a decade, and then finally, the two words that I keep avoiding (why so simple and why so hard to say?): "I'm gay." And more than likely the girls already know but when I claim it, the thing I have so long not accepted, that is a revelation of another order. So simple and yet so hard, and so many years that have traveled from my heart to my mouth. I tell her of the boy in my Episcopal high school who was teased and kicked and spit on and called a fag until he went home one day and hanged himself. I tell her then of my great concern: as a new priest will it be a challenge for me to live my authentic life.

She speaks then.

"Now I know why God brought you here," she says. This stops me and she looks at me like she's heard all she needs to hear. The chipped cement picnic table with shards of broken tile set into it is between us. She seems to no longer care about the film crew.

"Why?" I ask, curious to understand the riddle of all this myself.

"God brought you here," she says, "Because you, of all people, understand us, you know us..." She says this all quite emphatically as a cockroach crawls over my sandal. And there it is, clear and as emphatic as the heat of Honduras, the startling realization that I am as uncomfortable with the label "gay" as the girls are with "orphan." How they never liked it when I said it, how they hated the word *orfanato* and preferred *hogar* which means home. Gay or orphan made us different. Made people whisper. Made people laugh. Made people pity. Made people

40

throw us away. The picnic table starts to feel like an altar.

"Really?" I question her declarative statement somewhat incredulously. Would my erudite liberal Yale professors, so well-versed on social justice matters, honestly believe me with a straight face if I told them I understand abandoned and abused Honduran girls better than anyone?

"Really," she says, matter-of-factly as a psychiatrist might. She's quite certain of it, and if she knows one thing, she definitely knows something of God and what God has done. The girl does not know her own story, or so I am told. Maybe she's blocked it out. From whence does this compassionate insight into me come? Could it be that she is giving me what all the seminaries and all the professors in the world could never give me? A pure and unadulterated and nonjudgmental acceptance, in short, a place.

"How do you know?" I ask, having had decades of feeling not a part of much.

And she, pausing, then tenderly, with confidence: "I've been watching you." So, I had been watched. We sit there for a time, fixed, tears in my eyes and a few in hers. The film crew is silent. But she goes further. She tells me it is all okay. Soothingly. She tells me that it's okay I'm gay and it's okay I am a priest. I weep more deeply then. That's when the world flips and she's the priest and I the supplicant.

I'm going to call that my real ordination, for it has come to mean more to me than the churchy affair that occurred a year prior with correct stole colors and lines read off programs, everyone genuflecting, shaking hands and giving out cards. From that night forward I start to feel less like I need to apologize for my existence. Not always, but much more. Isn't that, after all, what an ordination is for? Preparing to send a person out. Send me out she certainly did. Send me out with a collar around my neck instead of a noose. Send me out to do God's work.

...

I will leave Our Little Roses and raise over $100,000 to make the film, not the whole budget but a third. Unlike poems, where all you need is a pencil, films take money. I will go from church to church, from DC to Jackson Hole, from St. Louis to Martha's Vineyard, from Miami to Minnesota, and everywhere I go I will speak of the girl in the well. People will give generously and donations come from surprising sources. A Williams college student will write me a $20 check, and in Tequesta, Florida a man who owns T-shirt factories in San Pedro Sula secretly hands me a check for $10,000, saying, "Keep doing what you are doing."

The summer after I'd raised the money for the film, I naively took the manuscript to New York publishing houses, assuming that with my poetic credentials getting a book of poems by Honduran girls published would be easy. Everyone rejects it. The relentless heat of New York City bears down on me. Can't give up. Won't give up. Smart New York editors say, "We don't do that kind of stuff," and "Doesn't sell," and "Why is there so much violence there?" And yet another says, "Why not make a calendar of their art? You could do it yourself." Sharon Olds at dinner, one night, will tell me, when I am completely deflated and exhausted, my clothes wet with sweat, "Of course it's not going to get taken easily, it's an anthology by teenage girls!" Don't I understand how misogynistic the whole publishing industry and world is? I guess I do not.

Over the following couple of years, the book will get rejected at least forty to fifty times before I meet Luis J. Rodríguez accidentally in Los Angeles. I am asked to speak on a panel at the Los Angeles Times Festival of Books at the University of Southern California (USC) about poetry and politics for which I feel inappropriately selected. I don't understand why I am going, but a plane ticket and a hotel are offered and I say yes. The event takes place in a basement with less than twenty people.

People get up and leave before it even starts. Not promising. Luis is on the panel with me. We don't know each other. When my turn comes I do the only thing I can think to do: I start talking about the girls and the girl found in the well. The minute I open my mouth about the girls I feel him next to me getting quiet. And then he speaks after me and I learn that he founded and runs Tía Chucha Press in Los Angeles, based in the second largest Mexican and Central American community in the US, a press that has published the first books of many now well-known poets that got rejected everywhere else, including distinguished African American voices like Elizabeth Alexander, Terrance Hayes, and A. Van Jordan. And then I know what to do next. I ask him to have coffee with me and ask him to consider the book. He says he will. The whole time I'll feel the girls standing behind me. I will constantly feel that I can't let them down. The whole project, book and film, will take seven years to complete.

An anonymous philanthropist will donate a yearly poetry residency at Our Little Roses, so the work of poetry can continue in the home. So the book you now hold is not only made from my efforts but those of the poets: Rebecca Watkins, Luis J. Rodríguez, and his wife Trini Rodríguez. Thus with some of the poems you will notice the age of the girls change depending on the year they are taught. More visiting teachers of poetry are on their way. More poets will sit in the carved chair.

But perhaps the most surprising result of all this is that the founder, Diana Frade, recently told me that Aylin is coming to chapel every morning and saying that she wants to be a poet, she knows it won't be easy, that she'll need to study something else, she says, but it's the only thing she wants to do. My friend and fellow poet, Richard Blanco, sponsors her.

...

I haven't seen that girl who sat with me on the bench with the film crew in several years. And the scene was cut from the film. The editor felt it was too weighted and focused on me when what we all wanted in the end was a film focused on those girls. The final cut dazzlingly focuses on them and it is my hope this book achieves a similar effect. But often that scene hangs there in my mind. The film, called "Voices Beyond the Wall," executive produced by James Franco, makes the film-festival rounds in 2017.

Often, during my church-work days in Madrid, I think of that girl. I see her on Facebook. I learn that she got pregnant, and on the same day I finish this introduction, she bears her child. A healthy baby boy, born on May 7th, 2017, Mother's Day in Spain. Not married I don't think. I hear she went to work in a call center. What happens, I wonder, when the call comes in to her cubicle, in the sea of cubicles, in San Pedro Sula? "Where are you from?" an American white woman will ask with some irritation. She will have detected just the slightest accent perhaps. I imagine the tone of the American white woman to be unconsciously entitled. She won't mean to be insulting or impatient, but she will be. I've heard that tone a thousand times and I've borne the same tone myself in the past, now to my own regret. I imagine her undocumented Latina maid mopping in the background raising her eyebrows when the American woman can't see her. And the girl whom I taught, found in the well—the blue mountains behind her, the mangoes swinging so delicately on their fragile stems—will respond, "Honduras. San Pedro Sula, Honduras."

—*Spencer Reece*
Día de la Madre
7 de mayo, 2017
Catedral del Redentor
Madrid, Spain

POEMS

Little Rose

AYLIN, AGE 16

Little Rose, please close your beautiful eyes.
I can no longer bear to see the pain inside of them,
the pain caused by what I couldn't prevent.

Rosita

AYLIN, 16 AÑOS

Rosita, por favor cierra tus lindos ojos.
Ya no aguanto seguir viendo el dolor que llevan dentro,
un dolor causado por lo que yo no pude prevenir.

Ancestors

9TH GRADE CLASS, 2013

My grandpa, he owns a bakery which has helped our family for a long time.

My great grandmother didn't care what people said; she was a fighter.

My great-great grandmother lived to be 103 and worked as a domestic close to the train station. She sold food to workers that went to the station. The train was used solely for transportation of food and farming equipment. She was a hard worker. Everyone was sustained by her income. She married and was then called Doña Santos Molina and had one son and four daughters. Doña Santos Molina left home and she had to take care of everyone. When she died they named the town after her.

My grandfather passed away last year and I was really sad. He lived in a little town called Tocoa. I didn't get to spend time with him. Some people say he was from El Salvador but he wouldn't tell. He knew magic because his uncle was a magician. He had a wife named Rosa. Sometimes he told me stories about Honduras and how it used to be.

Los antepasados

Mi abuelo, él tiene una panadería que ha ayudado a nuestra familia por mucho tiempo.

A mi bisabuela no le importaba lo que decía la gente; ella tenía un espíritu luchador.

Mi tatarabuela vivió hasta los 103 años y era obrera doméstica cerca de la estación de trenes. Ella vendía comida a los trabajadores que iban a la estación. El tren era sólo para la transportación de comida y equipamiento de granja. Ella era muy trabajadora. Todos fueron sostenidos por sus ingresos. Ella se casó y luego se llamó Doña Santos Molina y tuvo un hijo y cuatro hijas. Doña Santos Molina se fue de su casa y tuvo que cuidar y proveer para todos. Cuando ella murió nombraron el pueblo por ella.

Mi abuelo falleció el año pasado y me puse muy triste. El vivió en un pueblito llamado Tocoa. Yo no pude pasar tiempo con él. Unos dicen que era de El Salvador pero él nunca dijo si era verdad. El sabía magia porque su tío era un mago. Su esposa se llamaba Rosa. A veces me contaba historias de Honduras y cómo solía ser.

I was Six Years Old

KATHERINE, AGE 15

We live in a world that's full of hate.
I live in *Pequeñas Rosas* in Honduras

that is why I am close to *El Bordo*,
a place that is one of the most dangerous,

because they kill you, attack women and follow
you when you aren't looking.

My name is Katherine and I am fifteen years old.
My mother is dead and I never knew my father.

At the age of six, I came here. I felt I was in
paradise, but I missed my family even though

I knew this was safer for me. In this place
we live behind a giant wall. I hope that the world

will know of my life in this place and people
realize what they have. I do not think

you realize the violence we live in.

Tenía seis años

KATHERINE, 15 AÑOS

Vivimos en un mundo lleno de odio.
Vivo en Pequeñas Rosas en Honduras,

por lo que estoy cerca de El Bordo.
Este lugar es uno de los más peligrosos

porque matan, violan mujeres e incluso asaltan
sin que uno se dé cuenta que la persiguen.

Mi nombre es Katherine y tengo quince años.
Mi madre murió y a mi padre nunca lo conocí.

Tenía seis años cuando llegué aquí. Sentí que estaba
en un paraíso, pero extrañaba a mi familia

aunque sabía que estaba más segura aquí. En este lugar
vivimos detrás de un gran muro. Espero que el mundo

sepa de mi vida en este lugar y se den cuenta de todo
lo que tienen. Pienso que no se han dado cuenta

de la violencia en que vivimos.

Slow Motion

ANA RUTH, AGE 17

I am a camera although people think I am a sloth.

A cámara lenta

ANA RUTH, 17 AÑOS

Soy una cámara aunque la gente piensa que soy
una perezosa.

To My Books

DIANA, AGE 18

My books are always with me:
Me Before You, The Fault in Our Stars.

My books help place me in a random world:
Reached, Matched, Crossed, and *Graceling.*

Whenever I feel sad
I just open my books:

Thin Space and *The Selection.*
My books are always by my side.

My books never let me down:
The Mortal Instruments and *After.*

I never get bored with my books:
Leah and *My Life is a Disaster.*

They are my dogs! My books, my books—
The Spectacular Now.

I can't get rid of them.

Por mis libros

DIANA, 18 AÑOS

Mis libros siempre están conmigo:
Me Before You, The Fault in Our Stars,

Mis libros ayudan a situarme en un mundo aleatorio:
Reached, Matched, Crossed, y Graceling.

Cuando quiera que me sienta triste
solamente abro mis libros:

Thin Space y *The Selection.*
Mis libros están siempre a mi lado.

Mis libros nunca me decepcionan:
The Mortal Instrument y *After.*

Yo nunca me aburro de mis libros:
Leah y *My Life is a Disaster.*

Son mis fieles compañeros. Mis libros, mis libros—
The Spectacular Now.

No puedo deshacerme de ellos.

The Shepherd

BIANCA, AGE 16

In the mountains
of Santa Barbara,
he passes time alone.

His sixty-three sheep
are soft like pillows.
They are vulnerable.

Wind blows songs
in his ears; the wind
disappears like seconds

of a clock. His work
is difficult because
he is alone. He is like

Belkis, the *tía* in our home.
I'm one of those sheep.

El pastor

BIANCA, 16 AÑOS

En las montañas
de Santa Bárbara
él pasa mucho tiempo solo.

Sus sesenta y tres ovejas
son suaves como almohadas.
Ellas son vulnerables.

El viento sopla canciones
en sus oídos; el viento
desaparece como segundos

en un reloj. Su trabajo
es difícil porque
está solo. Él es como

Belkis, la tía en nuestro hogar.
Yo soy una de esas ovejas.

Invisible for All My Life

PAOLA, AGE 18

I am an eighteen-year-old girl.
This girl has put up with being invisible all her life.
She didn't ask to be the happiest woman in the world
but she did ask for someone to take care of her.

She never had the opportunity to have a family,
to receive love which is the only thing she wanted.

I don't know if I'm in this world with love
or only that they were obligated to bring me into it.
It is awful to know you are a throw away child.

I feel a hole in my soul and I don't know how to fill it.
I know there are people that love me,
but is it true love?
Sometimes I wonder, I have had many opportunities
    to die...
Why didn't I die in those moments?

Life doesn't make much sense if there is no LOVE!!!

Invisible toda mi vida

PAOLA, 18 AÑOS

Soy una chava de dieciocho años
que ha soportado ser invisible toda su vida.
Ella no pidió ser la mujer más feliz del mundo
pero sí que alguien cuidara de ella.

Ella nunca tuvo la oportunidad de tener
una familia que le brindara amor, lo cual
era lo único que ella quería.

No sé si estoy en este mundo con amor
o porque les obligaron a traerme.
Es feo saber que eres una hija rechazada.

Siento un vacío en mi alma y no sé cómo llenarlo.
Sé que hay personas que me quieren
pero, ¿será ese un amor verdadero?
A veces me pregunto, tuve muchas oportunidades
    de morir…
¿Por qué no morí en esos momentos?

¡¡¡La vida no tiene sentido si no hay AMOR!!!

My Honduras

ASTRID, AGE 17

This is my Honduras.
Some people run away from my home.
It makes me happy
because they have a better life.

But my country?
Who is listening to the sound of my sea?
Who is exploring my beautiful country?
Who is seeing the beauty of my green mountains?

Who is paying attention to my message?
My home is full of memories
where I was born and where I learned
no matter what

you have to go on with your life.
I still don't know my future.
I still don't know my way.
But remember this of me:

I will always love my country.

Mi Honduras

ASTRID, 17 AÑOS

Esta es mi Honduras.
Algunas personas huyen de mi hogar.
Me hace sentir feliz
porque tienen una vida mejor.

¿Pero mi país?
¿Quién está escuchando el sonido de mi mar?
¿Quién está explorando mi hermosa patria?
¿Quién está mirando la belleza de mis montañas verdes?

¿Quién le está prestando atención a mi mensaje?
Mi hogar está lleno de memorias
donde nací yo, y donde aprendí
no importa lo que pase

tú tienes que seguir con tu vida.
Todavía no sé mi futuro.
Todavía no conozco mi camino.
Pero recuerda esto de mí:

Siempre amaré a mi país.

Waterfall

AYLIN, AGE 16

Waterfall, waterfall, wash my sins away.
Waterfall, waterfall, make the pain go away.
Waterfall, waterfall, make me forget.
Waterfall, waterfall, make me drown in your
   precious waters.
Make me drown so I can no longer feel
the ferocity of my flesh being peeled
by the real me that is so tired of hiding inside.
Waterfall, waterfall, have mercy on me.

Cascada

AYLIN, 16 AÑOS

Cascada, cascada, límpiame de mis pecados.
Cascada, cascada, quítame el dolor.
Cascada, cascada, ayúdame a olvidar.
Cascada, cascada, ahógame en tus bellas aguas.
Ahógame, para que ya no pueda sentir
la ferocidad de mi carne siendo pelada
por la verdadera yo que está tan cansada de
    esconderse dentro.
Cascada, cascada, ten piedad de mí.

I am an Ant

RICCY, AGE 17

I am an ant feeling scared.
Someone might step on me!
Destroy all my dreams!
I am an ant and I know
the world is bothered
most of the time by the way
I look. I am an ant befriending
the other world. I am an ant
that is walking along
with no one beside me.

Soy una hormiga

RICCY, 17 AÑOS

Soy una hormiga asustada.
¡Alguien podría aplastarme!
¡Harían pedazos todos mis sueños!
Soy una hormiga, y sé
que con frecuencia al mundo
le molesta mi aspecto.
Soy una hormiga que se hace
amiga del otro mundo.
Soy una hormiga
que camina sin nadie a mi lado.

Some Lists

10TH GRADE, 2013

What are my nicknames?

I have a lot of nicknames: Dumbo; Duck Butt; Airplane; Elf; Chicken; Four-Eyes.

What are my responsibilities?

My homework; pray; give food to my gerbil.

What do I see from my bed?

I see the ceiling; the door; the wall—I see the other girls sleeping.

My possessions?

My toothbrush; my clothes; my shoes; my bed; my closet; my towel; my school supplies; my uniform.

Names I am called:

Negra; Pirata; Hipopótama; Esclava; Celia Cruz; Niggah; Whale; Pig; Cookie.

What is in the Air?

Oxygen; carbon dioxide; birds; airplanes; the sky; clouds; sounds; people; smoke.

Algunas listas

CLASE DE 10º GRADO, 2013

¿Cuáles son mis apodos?

Yo tengo muchos apodos: Dumbo, Cola de Pato; Avión; Duende; Gallina; la Cuatro Ojos.

¿Cuáles son mis responsabilidades?

Mi tarea; orar; darle comida a mi jerbo.

¿Qué veo desde mi cama?

Veo al techo; la puerta; la pared — veo a las otras chicas durmiendo.

¿Mis posesiones?

Mi cepillo de dientes; mi ropa; mis zapatos; mi cama; mi armario; mi toalla; mis materiales escolares; mi uniforme.

¿Los nombres que me llaman?

Negra; Pirata; Hipopótama; Esclava; Celia Cruz; Niggah; Ballena; Cerda; Galleta.

¿Qué está en el aire?

Oxígeno; dióxido de carbono; pájaros; aviones; el cielo; nubes; sonidos; gente; humo.

I will be a Happy Girl

LEYLI, AGE 16

When I look up at the sky my world is white. The wind blows the clouds. I want the world to be blue, like the ocean across the street in my imagination. I want my life to be fun like the girls I hear around on the street. My name is long and complicated. I don't know who gave me my name. I don't like my name. It is difficult to write. I would like to be a psychologist because I would like to help many people. I do not have brothers or sisters. I have parents but I have not seen them in a long time. When I was six I saw my parents a few times, between one and four in the afternoon. I forgot their names. When I look up at the sky I do not wonder about them. I am going to play and I am going to dance to have some fun with the dark shadows. I will be a happy girl.

Seré una niña fcliz

LEYLI, 16 AÑOS

Cuando miro al cielo mi mundo es blanco. El viento sopla
las nubes. Quiero que mi mundo sea azul, como el océano
al lado de la calle en mi imaginación. Quicro que mi vida
sea feliz como las niñas que oigo cn la calle. Mi nombre
es largo y complicado. No sé quién me dio este nombre.
No me gusta mi nombre. Es difícil escribir. Quiero ser
psicóloga porque me gustaría ayudar a mucha gente. Yo
no tengo hermanas ni hermanos. Yo tengo padres pero no
los he visto desde hace mucho tiempo. Cuando tenía seis
años vi a mis padres unas cuantas veces, entre la una y las
cuatro de la tarde. Se me olvidaron sus nombres. Cuando
miro hacia el cielo no me pregunto acerca de ellos. Voy a
jugar y a bailar para divertirme en las sombras oscuras.
Seré una niña feliz.

Metaphor

DIANA, AGE 18

People think I'm shy
because I'm quiet.
I am the wind because
I want to be free.

Metáfora

DIANA, 18 AÑOS

La gente cree que soy tímida
porque soy callada.
Soy el viento porque
quiero ser libre.

A Honduran Story

KATHERINE, AGE 15

Look at Jennifer and Bryan kiss
at the Church of San Pablo!
The church looks like a toy.
They met in third grade.
Her hands sweat like crazy
because she's lived in a home
for girls without parents
and she's rarely seen boys.
She gets pregnant,
and they will now marry.
That's how things go here.
Yes, she looks like a fat frog.
When Jennifer helps Bryan
button his pants at the wedding,
the button flies towards her eye
and Jennifer loses her eyeball.
These things happen here.
Three weeks later, Jennifer asks
for a divorce, she has her son
and they live under the bridge.
One day her son falls into the river.
The river is the color of a knife
and the river takes him.
I'm telling all of you,
if you come here
this could happen to your life.

Una historia hondureña

KATHERINE, 15 AÑOS

¡Mira como Jennifer y Bryan se besan
en la Iglesia de San Pablo!
La iglesia parece de juguete.
Ellos se conocieron en tercer grado.
Sus manos sudan como locas,
porque ella ha vivido en un hogar
para niñas sin padres
y rara vez ha visto chicos.
Ella se ha embarazado
y se van a casar.
Así es como son las cosas aquí.
Sí, ella parece una rana gorda.
Cuando Jennifer ayuda a Bryan
a abrocharse los pantalones en la boda,
el botón vuela hacia su ojo
y Jennifer pierde el ojo.
Estas cosas pasan aquí.
Tres semanas después, Jennifer pide
el divorcio, ella tiene su hijo
y viven bajo un puente.
Un día su hijo se cae en el río.
El río es el color de un cuchillo,
y el río se lo lleva.
Les aviso a todos,
si vienen aquí,
esto les podría pasar a su vida.

Little Red Hot Lips

ANA RUTH, AGE 15

Little Red Hot Lips went away, la la!
Off to her beloved grand mama!
She knew nothing about life at all,
nothing about anything outside the wall.

Little Red Hot Lips went on her way,
dressed in red with lots of hairspray,
packing up her iPod on the way
listening to Rihanna sing "Stay."

Oh Little Red Hot Lips, la la la la!
Saw the wolf and he saw her. Ta da!
Her heart went thump-thump-thump
for the black-eyed wolf she met at the dump.

Pobrecita! They found Little Red Hot Lips
with scars and blood on her chest and hips!
Nothing more dangerous than this:
the black-eyed creature she'd kissed.

Caperucita de labios pintados de rojo

ANA RUTH, 15 AÑOS

Caperucita con labios pintados de rojo salió, ¡la la!
¡para ir a ver a su querida abuela!
No sabía nada de la vida
nada de nada fuera del muro.

Caperucita con labios pintados de rojo salió en camino,
vestida de rojo con un montón de laca,
con su iPod prendido
escuchando a Rihanna cantando "Stay".

Oh Caperucita con labios pintados de rojo, ¡la la la la!
Ella vio al lobo y él la vio a ella. ¡Tá dá!
Su corazón latía ¡pum pum pum!
por el lobo de ojos negros que conoció en el basurero.

¡Pobrecita! ¡encontraron a Caperucita con labios
    pintados de rojo
con cicatrices y sangre en el pecho y las caderas!
Nada más peligroso que esto:
la criatura de ojos negros que había besado.

Beauty & the Beast

Ana Cecilia, age 15

There once was a girl from Progreso. She was beautiful,
had green eyes and long black hair and soft skin. Her skin
was soft as cotton. She looked like a model. One day she
was working as a waitress in a restaurant named Rico's.
She went to take an order of baleadas from a really hand-
some guy. He looked like a movie star. He was tall and
had brown hair, blue eyes, and his skin was bronze-col-
ored. His voice sounded like a lion. She was carrying her
café con leche and stared at him. She was hypnotized.
She tripped and fell. He laughed at her and picked her
up. He introduced himself and said his name was Fabian.
The days passed and they began dating. He brought her
flowers and chocolates and took her to Islas de la Bahía.
After they knew each other for two months he got on
drugs. He became a gang member in Mara 18. He got tat-
toos and said mean things. He said she was stupid. He did
not pay attention to her. He killed a family and went to
jail in San Pedro Sula. She went to visit him at the jail and
it smelled like piss. They separated but she got pregnant.
She went to work in a factory and raised her son who she
named Lloyd. She moved to Islas de la Bahía. She thinks
often about love and what the meaning of it is. Some-
times she thinks love is like torture. And sometimes, when
she sits at her kitchen table, all alone, she thinks: I don't
have that beast anymore.

La bella y la bestia

Ana Cecilia, 15 años

Hace mucho tiempo había una niña de Progreso. Era guapa, tenía los ojos verdes, el pelo largo y negro, piel suave. Su piel era tan suave como el algodón. Parecía un modelo. Un día estaba trabajando como camarera en un restaurante que se llamaba Rico's. Fue a tomar una orden de baleadas de un chico muy guapo. Parecía una estrella de cine. Era alto con cabello castaño, ojos azules y su piel era de color bronce. Su voz era como la de un león. Ella llevaba su café con leche y lo miraba fijamente. Estaba hipnotizada. Se tropezó y cayó. Él se echó a reír y la levantó. Se presentó a sí mismo y le dijo que se llamaba Fabián. Pasaron los días y empezaron a salir. Le regalaba flores y bombones y la llevó a Las Islas de la Bahía. Después de dos meses él empezó a usar drogas. Él se hizo miembro de una pandilla, la Mara 18. Se tatuó y la ofendía. Le decía que era una estúpida. No le hacía caso. Mató a una familia y fue a la cárcel en San Pedro Sula. Ella fue a visitarlo a la cárcel que olía a orín. Ellos se separaron pero ella quedó embarazada. Empezó a trabajar en una fábrica y crió a su hijo que lo llamó Lloyd. Se fue a vivir a Las Islas de la Bahía. Ella piensa muchas veces en el amor y en su significado. A veces piensa que el amor es una tortura. Y a veces, cuando se sienta en la mesa de su cocina sola, piensa: Ya no tengo a esa bestia.

The Walls

Leyli, age 17

Sometimes I wonder if I can paint these walls
with my thoughts.

Then I wonder if my thoughts are strong enough
to hold up the walls.

The walls are mostly white but I paint them
all the time in my head.

Often happiness comes after I examine them:
I belong here.

Los muros

LEYLI, 17 AÑOS

En ocasiones me pregunto si podría pintar estos muros
con mis pensamientos.

Y luego me pregunto si mis pensamientos son
lo bastante fuertes como para sostener estos muros.

Los muros son por lo general blancos, pero
en mi cabeza los pinto sin cesar.

Me siento feliz cuando los veo: yo pertenezco aquí.

A Prayer for Ilda

ISMELDA, AGE 16

Tonight I am in my green room.
Four girls are here with me.
Tonight I think of Ilda, my sponsor.

You were 27 and tall as a palm tree.
Your laugh sounded like the ocean,
it was calm like when little waves tickle the shore.

You loved me and came to visit me once
for three hours under the cancha's tin roof.

Ilda, I haven't seen you in ten years.
I wonder where you are in the USA.
You left to find work and money
for your family. I miss you, Ilda.
My dad told me you came back
to construct an elegant white house.
You didn't come to see me.
Sometimes I think you forgot about me.

This prayer is a house for you.
This prayer is a dinner for you
with pizza, Coke, and ice cream.
Come visit me soon, Ilda.
I will be waiting for you behind the big walls.
Tell Don Julio to let you in.
You will find me in my green room.

Una oración para Ilda

ISMELDA, 16 AÑOS

Esta noche estoy en mi habitación verde.
Cuatro chavas están aquí conmigo.
Esta noche pienso en Ilda, mi madrina.

Tenías 27 años y eras tan alta como una palmera.
Tu risa sonaba como el océano,
era calmado como cuando las olitas cosquillan a la orilla
    del mar.

Me querías y viniste a visitarme una vez
por tres horas debajo de la azotea de la cancha.

Ilda, hace diez años que no te veo.
Me pregunto dónde estás en EEUU.
Te fuiste para buscar trabajo y dinero
para tu familia. Te extraño, Ilda.
Mi papá me dijo que regresaste
para construir una casa blanca y elegante.
No viniste a verme.
A veces pienso que me has olvidado.

Esta oración es una casa para ti.
Esta oración es una cena para ti
con pizza, coca y helado.
Ven a verme pronto, Ilda.
Te estaré esperando detrás de los grandes muros.
Dile a Don Julio que te deje entrar.
Me encontrarás en mi habitación verde.

Counting

AYLIN, AGE 15

Every week, every day, every hour, every minute, and
every second that I pass without my family it feels like a
knife trying to get inside a rock. I am the knife and the
rock is my life. So this is me, Aylin, and this is my diffi-
cult life without my family. Some people think that liv-
ing in a home for girls like Our Little Roses is a big
blessing. Yes, I say to those people, it is a great blessing
but at the same time it is a curse. Every night I start
thinking and talking to God in my prayers, "Why, God,
why did my family leave me alone?" There is no answer.
A lot of people see me with my sisters and my aunt,
who is not really my aunt, and they think we are a
happy group, but really all of us think the same thing
that no one ever says: One day, will our mother come to
visit us? It is ugly to know that everyone in this school
is celebrating Mother's Day. On this day, I feel ashamed
to be me. But, God, listen to this: I am counting time
like people count stars and I will keep counting until
my mother comes. My sisters are graduating and soon I
will go to college too. When I graduate from college
and when I am finally somebody in this world, God, I
will go straight to Mexico where my mother lives and I
will stare at her like I stare at the stars and with a voice
that cracks like thunder I will say: I FORGIVE YOU! But
for now, God, I am here, in Our Little Roses, counting.

Contando

AYLIN, 15 AÑOS

Cada semana, cada día, cada hora, cada minuto y cada se-
gundo que la paso sin mi familia parece un cuchillo
tratando de penetrar una roca. Yo soy el cuchillo y la roca
es mi vida. Así que esta soy yo, Aylin, y esta es mi vida
difícil sin mi familia. Algunas personas piensan que vivir
en un hogar para niñas como Nuestras Pequeñas Rosas es
una bendición. Sí, le digo a esas personas, es una gran
bendición pero al mismo tiempo es una maldición. Cada
noche empiezo a pensar y a hablar con Dios en mis ora-
ciones, ¿Dios, por qué mi familia me abandonó? ¿Por qué?
No hay respuesta. Muchas personas me ven con mis her-
manas y mi tía, que no es mi verdadera tía, y piensan que
somos un grupo feliz, pero todos pensamos lo mismo, lo
que nadie quiere decir: ¿algún día nuestra madre vendrá a
visitarnos? Es feo saber que todos en la escuela están cele-
brando El Día de la Madre. En este día, me siento aver-
gonzada de mí misma. Pero Dios escucha esto: estoy
contando el tiempo como las personas cuentan las estrel-
las y voy a seguir contando hasta que mi madre venga.
Mis hermanas ya se están graduando y pronto yo también.
Y cuando me gradúe del colegio y cuando finalmente sea
alguien en este mundo, Dios, voy a ir a México donde vive
mi madre y voy a quedarme mirándola como cuando miro
las estrellas y con una voz que truena como un relámpago
le diré: ¡YO TE PERDONO! Pero por el momento, Dios,
estoy aquí, en Nuestras Pequeñas Rosas, contando.

Soon

Anonymous, age 17

I am seventeen
and in two months
I will be eighteen.
Soon I am leaving
this place called
Nuestras Pequeñas Rosas.
I left Honduras once.
I went to Philadelphia.
My biggest dream is
to be a flight attendant
in the USA.
I want to explore the world.
This place is my home
and it has meant
everything to me.
What is home for you?
Your school can be your home
even if you don't have a bed.
Living here has been like
tasting cotton candy:
it is that sweet.
My family is made up
of the people that love
and support me.

I will miss Doña Diana
because she is like a mother
to me. That is the truth.
My real story is a chronicle
of charity. I will never
forget this place I call home.
Honduras, I prefer the visions
of your green mountains.
I am not sure if the world
will love me like in this place.
What will the world
expect from me?

Pronto

ANÓNIMA, 17 AÑOS

Tengo diecisiete años
y en dos meses
tendré dieciocho.
Pronto voy a salir
de este lugar que se llama
Nuestras Pequeñas Rosas.
Salí de Honduras una vez.
Fui a Filadelfia.
Mi sueño más grande es
ser aeromoza
en EEUU.
Quiero explorar el mundo.
Este lugar es mi hogar
y ha significado
todo para mí.
¿Qué es un hogar para ti?
Tu escuela puede ser tu casa
incluso si no tienes una cama.
Vivir aquí es como
saborear algodón dulce:
es así de dulce.
Mi familia está formada
por personas que me quieren
y me apoyan.

Voy a extrañar a Doña Diana
porque es como una madre
para mí. Esa es la verdad.
Mi historia real es una crónica
de caridad. No olvidaré
este lugar que llamo hogar.
Honduras, prefiero las vistas
de tus montañas verdes.
No estoy segura
si el mundo me va
a querer como en este lugar.
¿Qué esperará
el mundo de mí?

For All to See

7TH GRADE, 2013

Para the driver who has worked here twelve sweaty, damp
years and was an orphan;
Para the guards, the *Catrachos*, who are big strong heroes
who protect the girls
(one is missing an eye);
Para the gangs, who brag who they will kill with their
weapons, but sometimes,
they, too, do good things for their families. Some are poor,
very poor;
Para the teachers who are like books, full of blue wisdom;
Para the students who stroll in their hot halls;
Para the ladies who clean the school behind the razor
wire;
Para me who lives in this city and who likes this country
where they make the best *baleadas;*
Para you who are reading this poem, we just want to tell
you thank you
for reading this, it is for all the people who don't know
Honduras.

Para que todos lo vean

CLASE DE 7º GRADO, 2013

Para el conductor que ha trabajado aquí durante doce
   sudorosos húmedos años y era huérfano,
Para los guardias, los Catrachos, que son grandes héroes
   fuertes que protegen a las chavas (a uno le falta un ojo),
Para las pandillas, que se jactan de quien van a matar,
   con sus armas, pero a veces, también hacen cosas
   buenas por sus familias. Algunos también
   son pobres, muy pobres,
Para los profesores que son como libros, llenos de
   sabiduría azul,
Para los alumnos que deambulan por los pasillos
   sofocantes,
Para las mujeres que limpian la escuela detrás de la
   serpentina de alambre de púas,
Para mí que vivo en esta ciudad y que quiere a este país
   donde se hacen las mejores baleadas,
Para ti que lees este poema, nosotros sólo queremos
   decirte gracias por leer este libro, es para toda la
   gente que no conoce a Honduras.

Rose

RICCI, AGE 14

This young
rose, it represents all of us here.
Careful! It is the prettiest young rose
we have: life needs love,
love needs life.

Rosa

RICCI, 11 AÑOS

Esta rosa
joven, nos representa a todos aquí.
¡Ten cuidado! Es la rosa joven más bonita
que tenemos: la vida necesita amor,
el amor necesita vida.

POSTSCRIPT

A Hidden History

BEAUTIFUL, lush, and vibrant, those are the words I think of when I think of Central America. The region contains some of the most hard-working and resilient people anywhere, rooted in rich traditions reaching back tens of thousands of years to Mayans, Nahuatl-speaking tribes, and other indigenous peoples. Their story includes the more recent Spanish conquistadors, African slaves, and migrants from all parts of Asia, the Middle East, and Europe.

Central America, to my mind, also exhibits what's wrong with modern society: money, prestige, and power are valued over the principles of cooperation and caring. Central Americans have not been provided with the tools and teachings (including their largely trampled ancestral knowledge) to be autonomous and free. With this misguided, post-colonial, broken pact as a backdrop, it comes as no surprise that Central America's Northern Triangle—El Salvador, Guatemala, and Honduras—has for more than 25 years been the world's most violent gang area. The disconnect between power and freedom has fueled wars that have devastated that region for far longer.

These three countries were hit by civil and proxy wars in the 1970s and 1980s. In El Salvador, more than 75,000 people were killed from 1980 to 1992. Guatemala lost 100,000 over forty years of struggle. And Honduras was caught in the Iran-Contra Affair from 1983 to 1986 during the Reagan years,

117

which used illegal sales of arms to Iran and the crack epidemic in inner-city America to bring arms and other resources to counter-revolutionaries (Contras) in Honduras against Nicaragua's Sandinista government. Although peace accords in El Salvador and Guatemala were signed in the early 1990s, no sooner did the ink dry than instability exploded again after the United States deported L.A.-based gang youth following the 1992 Los Angeles Uprising, the worst civil disturbance in the US in 50 years. A 1996 immigration act resulted in the deportation of more than a million people in twenty years who had purportedly committed crimes. Some deportees ended up in place like Cambodia and Armenia; the majority was sent to Mexico and Central America.

The alleged criminals and gang members deported to the Northern Triangle were mostly children of refugees who had escaped the civil wars. These refugees landed in the Pico-Union, Westlake, Koreatown, Hollywood, South L.A., and San Fernando Valley barrios. The trauma of US-financed wars met the trauma of inner city Los Angeles. Some of the Salvadorans, the largest Central American refugee group to these neighborhoods, joined long established Chicano (Mexican American) gangs, with roots in the children of refugees from the 1910-1930 Mexican Revolution and other upheavals that over the decades created *pachucos* and *cholos*. They joined 18th Street, one of Los Angeles largest street gangs, started by Chicanos in the 1960s that later recruited across nationalities, including non-Mexicans.

However, Salvadoran youth also created the Mara Salvatrucha (first known as Mara Stoners) in the 1980s. "Mara," tied to the Spanish word for soldier ants, was a Central American expression for any group of street youths. "Salvatrucha," meaning "wise Salvadorans," combined Chicano slang with a Salvi twist. This group first arose out of 18th Street, but soon broke away, leading to intense warfare with 18th Street and other street organizations. Youth from Guatemala and Honduras joined both gangs, along with newly arrived Mexicans who in the 1980s and 1990s fled Mexico's worst economic crisis since the Mexican Revolution.

Highly influenced by the Chicano *cholo* style, the Mara Salvatrucha (MS) made a reputation as a deadly gang and, like 18th Street, began to spread out beyond its original confines west and south of downtown Los Angeles. By 1993, MS became part of the larger Sureños prison-street gang structure, including 18th Street. Sureños unite all Chicano/Latino street gangs in southern California. MS added the number 13 to their name to announce this allegiance: "13" is tied to Sureño gangs; "14" is tied to Norteños, northern/central California Chicano gangs. They are now known as MS-13.

Unfortunately, the U.S. deportations unleashed highly sophisticated L.A-based gangs into El Salvador, Guatemala, Honduras, as well as parts of Mexico. They brought with them the fine-line black-and-gray tattoo styles of Chicano gangs, including their manner of dress, walk, and slang. L.A.-style barrio graffiti showed up on walls throughout these countries. Once there, both 18th Street and MS-13 recruited children of war and poverty, including many abandoned homeless youth. Over the years, these children of war and poverty, as opposed to deportees, have dominated MS-13 and 18th Street in Central America. Just as barrio gang youth were exported so was L.A.-style barrio warfare. This at first confounded, dismayed, and angered the local population. They had known war and violence for decades, but not like this: drive-by (and walk-by) shootings, paying *renta* (peddlers, microbus enterprises, and others were being extorted with a tax-to-do-business within newly carved-out gang territories), and crack sales.

Local *maras* made up of lost youth that spent their days sniffing glue and criminal *bandas,* including highly trained armed criminal groups, tried to fight the growing numbers of MS-13 and 18th Street gangs. Many joined them. US policies, supporting rich families and dictators, fueled the 1980s civil wars, creating around 3 million refugees from the Northern Triangle that fled into the United States. Now, US anti-immigrant policies, with deportations of gang youth from L.A. barrios, keep increasing the violence in places like Honduras.

...

I first found my way through Mexico, Nicaragua, and Honduras in the early 1980s as a journalist after working in daily and weekly newspapers, radio, and as a freelancer for various publications. I covered indigenous and *campesino* uprisings in Baja California and Oaxaca in Mexico. I traveled throughout Nicaragua. I ended up in two prisons, Sandinista government offices, poor barrios, and more. I was shot at by high velocity rifles and bombed twice (although not hurt) in southern Honduras when I tried to explore the highly resourced Contra camps. We discovered the Contras had US ordnance at their disposal. Soon the Iran-Contra Affair got exposed and became big news. I witnessed the dangers and intrigue linked to the CIA.

In 1993, I visited El Salvador with photojournalist Donna De Cesare after we won the Dorothea Lange-Paul Taylor Prize from the Center for Documentary Studies of Duke University. We covered the growing phenomena of MS-13 in El Salvador and in Los Angeles. We returned to El Salvador in 1996 to do more interviews and presentations, including in prisons. We took part that year in a "Salvadoran Youth Confronting Violence" conference in San Salvador that led to a peace accord between MS-13, 18th Street, various city mayors, the new National Police, priests, ministers, and others.

But the right-wing ARENA government at the time undermined this effort, leading to more warfare. Instead of bringing in jobs, training, drug treatment, and education—as was proposed—El Salvador in the early 2000s initiated *"Mano Dura"* and later *"Super Mano Dura"* (Iron Fist and Super Iron Fist) policies with more police and more prisons. Anti-gang death squads grew with names like *Sombra Negra* (Black Shadow) and *Angeles de Muerte* (Angels of Death). "Social cleansing" (the eradication of gang members, including by death) became common. The US government aided these efforts. US-based investors created a billion-dollar private security industry in El Salvador. As MS-13 and 18th Street, now known as Mara 18 or Barrio 18, spread to Guatemala and Honduras, so did violence, *mano dura* policies, and private security enterprises. Repression worsened everything.

In 2001 I visited Guatemala with a team from the Young Men's Christian Association Street Intervention Project, working with MS-13 and 18th Street gang youth. In 2007, I returned to Guatemala with two organizers from L.A.'s Homeboy Industries. We spoke with *maras*, did interviews on radio and in print, and addressed community gatherings. We visited two prisons, including a women's facility.

By then I had become a gang expert witness for asylum cases involving Salvadoran, Guatemalan, Honduran, and Mexican migrants. I have taken part in around 70 cases. Although most cases have been lost, these efforts helped change the way people look at gang violence: the youth were not acting in isolation, they were part of a larger neglect with the pervasive complicity of corrupt governments and police. I also grasped the immensely detrimental role played by the United States.

...

In 2012, I heard about a gang peace with MS-13 and Barrio 18 that began in a Salvadoran prison and soon spread to other prisons and poor neighborhoods. Aided by former FMLN guerilla leader Raúl Mijango and Monsignor Fabio Colindres, the initial reports of the peace showed violence declining significantly, from fourteen murders a day to five murders a day.

My relationship with Homies Unidos, led by former MS-13 gang leader Alex Sanchez, and other gang prevention/intervention groups in Los Angeles, going back in some cases to 40 years, helped prepare me for this work. I took part in gang truces between Chicano gangs in the 1970s through groups like End Barrio Warfare Coalition and *El Centro Del Pueblo*. When I moved to Chicago in 1985, I participated in poetry and arts work, teaching writing in prisons, juvenile lockups, and homeless shelters.

In Chicago, I also facilitated youth development/restorative justice work with organizers and mentors working with gangs tied to the "People" and "Folks" associations. These groups included Youth Struggling for Survival and the Increase the Peace

Network. Some of this work involved truces and/or intervention among major Mexican and Puerto Rican gangs (including Latin Kings, Two-Six Nation, Imperial Gangsters, Insane Spanish Cobras, Latin Maniac Disciples, La Raza, Insane Campbell Boys, Gangster Party People, and others). I went out to Los Angeles just after the 1992 Uprising to work with trucing efforts of the African American Crips and Bloods gangs, dealing with groups like Mothers ROC, Hands Across Watts, and Amer-I-Can. And I took part in gang peace conferences in California, Texas, Washington D.C., Chicago, and Kansas City, including with Barrios Unidos of Santa Cruz, CA.

From 2006 to 2008, with some 40 other gang interventionists, I helped create a "Community-based Gang Intervention Model" under the auspices of then Los Angeles City Councilperson Tony Cardenas (now US Congressman). Los Angeles adopted this model and I took it to Chicago and other US cities as well as Mexico, El Salvador, Guatemala, Argentina, and England. In 2010, when Ciudad Juarez, Mexico was the "murder capital of the world" (this was also where my family lived when I was born in El Paso, Texas), I presented aspects of that plan to slums, a prison, a juvenile hall, community organizations, poetry collectives, and more.

In the summer of 2012, I was part of a group of 11 urban peace leaders, researchers, and advocates to access and advise the MS-13/Barrio 18 peace process. We came from Los Angeles, San Francisco, Washington DC, New York, and London. We were part of the Transnational Advisory Group in Support of the Peace Process in El Salvador (TAGSPPES). Our team visited six Salvadoran prisons (one for women), and a juvenile detention facility. We also met with many MS-13 and Barrio 18 leaders. We encountered community leaders in various pro-youth organizations. We dialogued with government officials. By then the Left-wing FMLN had a president and other officials in public office. The gang peace proved to be the only thing to lower the violence, including when more than ten municipalities became Zones of Peace and Security whereby gang youth would not be harassed or attacked, and everyone worked for the betterment of those communities. Still, political pressure from the United States, among other pressures, ended up again pulling the plug on peace.

In 2013, I returned to San Salvador to speak at a gang conference hosted by the Organization of American States (OAS). However, TAGSPPES members were told not to mention the gang peace. OAS, funded in large part by the United States, were threatened with losing funds if we dared to say anything about any accord between gangs. We did address best practices in gang prevention and intervention, all valuable, but were still silenced on what was potentially the most powerful means to peace—gang members giving up arms and crime, and a real process in return to alleviate job insecurity, derelict housing, and lack of educational opportunities. In other words, strategic structural changes were needed for this peace to benefit not just gang members but the whole country. Instead, stronger suppression forced gangs to become entrenched and intractable. I saw this happen with Chicano/Latino and African American gangs in Los Angeles and Chicago. Gangs faced more prisons and police, but nothing in terms of ending poverty, drug treatment on demand, jobs retraining, healthy re-entry into communities, and transformative justice practices—things we know work when applied fully and consistently. The political will was simply not there.

Now, in 2017, El Salvador has the highest murder rate of any country in the world. Second is Honduras. Third Guatemala. Only parts of Mexico caught in drug cartel wars and war zones like Syria have worse levels of violence. This led to a new refugee crisis when between 2013 and 2015 some 100,000 unaccompanied minors fled the violence in the Northern Triangle to the United States.

...

I met Spencer Reece in the summer of 2016, an Episcopalian American priest and poet based in Madrid, Spain. Spencer and

I were on a poetry panel at the Los Angeles Times Festival of Books. He spoke about the abandoned girls of Our Little Roses Girl's Home in San Pedro Sula, Honduras, a city that by then had been designated the world's most violent. At one point, Spencer was in tears as he spoke of the poverty and daily violence surrounding these girls, but also how Our Little Roses became an oasis where he spent a year teaching poetry. As he read the girls' work, tears filled my eyes.

Immediately after the panel dispersed, Spencer invited me to teach poetry at Our Little Roses. He said there was an opportunity to go there before Christmas. I accepted. Upon arriving, I met the home's founder, Diana Frade, and her husband, Episcopal Bishop Leo Frade, two Americans who maintain the home and adjoining Holy Family Bilingual School at great sacrifice. My wife Trini also came to Honduras, teaching and guiding beside me. She later helped translate the girls' poems. She's a poet, former teacher, revolutionary thinker/activist, and practices Native spiritual healing. A Chicana, Trini was spiritually adopted 20 years ago by Dine (Navajo) elders Anthony and Delores Lee from Lukachukai, Arizona in the Navajo Nation.

In mid-November of 2016, Trini and I began our month-long work in a compound behind tall walls, with armed guards, in one of the poorest neighborhoods of San Pedro Sula: Villa Florencia. We worked with a group of eight girls of Our Little Roses on their writing. Simultaneously, we taught poetry in three or four classrooms a day, 4th to 11th grades, at Holy Family Bilingual School, organized by the school's director, Carlos Duarte.

We shared poetry books, including my own. We told our stories as Chicanos, both of us born and raised in the United States to Mexican migrant parents. How we grew up in poor working class barrios. We also spoke of how we maintained our Spanish against great odds, and how both of us struggled to master English. We then addressed the power of metaphor, the descriptive image, language that evokes, examines, and expresses. We exposed them to the writings of numerous poets helping them explore their own poetry. Towards the end, we chose three "winners" to read their writing at a celebration at

124

the Holy Family Bilingual School with parents and community members. The three, we assured everyone, were not better than anyone else, but best represented the students' overall writing. We returned all these writings to the teachers so they could continue the work we had started.

With the Our Little Roses girls, we met every Thursday and Friday afternoons. We also had outings with them into San Pedro Sula's center, graduation events, and to a retreat center in Pueblo Nuevo. Trini and I also visited the old San Fernando Fort and a beach on the Caribbean as well as the area around Lake Yojoa. The girls typed their work into our laptops. While some of them were shy at first, they opened up over the four weeks of writing sessions. All tried their best in English, some wrote in Spanish. Many exhibited an impressive understanding of the dynamics of poetry. In the end, to our surprise, students gave us hand-made cards, letters, and drawings. We felt honored.

...

Whether working with gangs or prisoners or the girls of Our Little Roses, poetry keeps shining light and hope in places shadowed by great neglect, disparities, and violence. That's why 28 years ago, I founded Tia Chucha Press in Chicago: to expand this hope—we've now published around 65 poetry collections, anthologies, a CD, and chapbooks. This is why Tia Chucha Press' editorial board agreed to publish Spencer Reece's book with his powerful and intimate essay and the poems of the girls from Spencer's workshops (as well as the workshops Trini and I, and Rebecca Watkins, facilitated). This book means more clarity in the world. Poetry reveals the soul like no other arrangement of words. People no one sees, or refuse to see, like gang youth or abused and abandoned girls, are for a moment on the page, seen, felt, understood—to that end, we, and Tia Chucha Press, dedicate our lives.

—*Luis J. Rodríguez*

AFTERWORD

Why Poetry?

WHEN I SET OUT to visit Our Little Roses in December of 2013 I didn't know what to expect. Well, that's not exactly true. Taking a look back now, I think I was expecting to find a solemn place filled with downtrodden girls, quiet and shy and head-bowed. Alongside Father Spencer Reece, I imagined my role would be that of the proverbial Good Samaritan—to be generous and kind to those less fortunate than me by teaching poetry in the spirit of service and social justice. While those were certainly virtuous intentions, from the moment I set foot inside the walls of the home it became apparent that there would be a whole lot more to my visit than I had expected.

Some of the girls were shy, but others were certainly not, asking me all sorts of delightfully personal questions: How old are you? Do you have a girlfriend? Do you speak Spanish? What car do you drive? And they equally shared their likes and dislikes without reservation. On the other hand, some were reserved, while others were flirty; some were fussy, others were totally easy-going; some were playful, others were moody. And all this changed minute by minute, depending on the weather, the time of day, and the day of the week. And, yes, there was laughter—plenty of it. Despite the tragic stories many of the girls harbored, they laughed and gossiped, played soccer, made pinkie swears, made-up each other's hair—and mine! Some were good, obedient students, others never did their assignments or would try to trick me into doing their homework for them. Some confessed they'd never seen their mother, some were angry, others at peace. They could hate. They could love. They could dream. They were teenage girls with a full spectrum of emotions.

How silly of me to have ever thought otherwise, to have over-simplified their lives in my mind. The girls ended up being my teachers—they taught me some very big lessons that I had forgotten. Life is a complex milieu of pain, loss, turmoil, but also triumph, laughter, and love. Each one of our stories is unique, yet at the heart of every story is our shared humanity. Everyone, whatever their walk in life, has something to offer the other. The girls' life stories and their very being renewed my faith in the resiliency of the human spirit. That wasn't what I was expecting when I arrived, but certainly what I took with me when I left.

And at the center of all this, their poetry which reflects all these dimensions of their lives. I'm often asked: Why poetry? Why is it important? Relevant? I have my standard-issue replies, noting how poetry makes us better readers, makes us pause and pay attention to the world; how it makes us see the extraordinary in the seemingly ordinary, opens our wounds and heals them, too. And most importantly, it urges us to be more aware, fulfilled human beings. All that's fine and dandy—and true. But now you and I both have living proof: the lives of these girls in twenty-two poems that you have just met through these pages. And if that's not important or relevant, then I don't know what is.

I continue to give my time and myself to Our Little Roses, not solely because the girls indeed are in need or merely because it's the "right thing to do." I give not because of what I have to offer, but more so, because of what the girls have to offer and teach the world about love, honesty, perseverance, and compassion, despite all they have been through, or rather, precisely because of all they have been through.

—*Richard Blanco*

ACKNOWLEDGMENTS

GRATEFUL ACKNOWLEDGMENT to the following publications:

Poetry: "I was Six Years Old," "The Shepherd," "Invisible for All My Life," "I Will be a Happy Girl," "A Honduran Story," "Little Red Hot Lips," "Beauty & the Beast," "A Prayer for Ilda," "For All to See," "Soon," and "Rose."

Rhino: "A Prayer for Ilda"

Publication of versions, or parts thereof, of "A Confession" appeared in: *What Did Jesus Ask*, edited by Elizabeth Dias, published by *Time* magazine, *The Anglican Theological Review*, and in *The American Poetry Review*.

I AM GRATEFUL to Iva Tičić, Soren Stockman, Sarah Humphries, Ralph Hamilton, Richard Blanco, Naomi Mulvihill, Jessie Auger, Lisa Schneier, Nicolaza Hernández, Gustavo Campos, Kenneth Stewart (in memoriam), Logan De La Cruz, Manuel Rodríguez Franco, Iñigo García Ureta, Carol Watson, Sheila Maldonado, Carlos Saavedra, James Franco, Betsy Franco, John Crowley, John Habich, Andrew Solomon, Bridget Chase (in memoriam), Alice Quinn and Mark Strand (in memoriam) for your help and encouragement as I worked on this book.

Deep gratitude to Mary Jane Zapp for your visit to Our Little Roses and the photographs you took that grace this book. You've helped us with Gwendolyn's request that the girls not be forgotten more than you will ever know.

And to the producers and crew of the 2017 documentary film "Voices Beyond the Wall: Twelve Love Poems from the Murder Capital of the World."

And finally, this book´s extended printing is made possible through the generosity of St. Mary Magdalene Episcopal Church and The Reverend Canon Mark Sims and Gail Haldeman, Ken Zapp and Cindy Kelley, and Art and Betsy Murphy. And special thanks to the Technoform Group of companies dedicated to children's education and long-term sustainable interests. Your support brings this book to the larger world and we cannot thank you enough for that.

BIOGRAPHIES

Spencer Reece is the author of *The Clerk's Tale* and *The Road to Emmaus*. He is the national secretary for the bishop of the Spanish Episcopal Church, Iglesia Española Reformada Episcopal, and lives in Madrid, Spain.

Marie Howe, state poet laureate of New York, is the author of *The Good Thief, What The Living Do, The Kingdom of Ordinary Time* and *Magdalene*. She edited the anthology *In the Company of My Solitude: American Writing from the AIDS Pandemic*. She lives in New York City, New York.

Luis J. Rodríguez, poet laureate of Los Angeles from 2014 to 2016, is founding editor of Tia Chucha Press and co-founder with Trini Rodríguez of Tia Chucha's Centro Cultural & Bookstore in the Northeast San Fernando Valley. He has authored 15 books in poetry, fiction, nonfiction, and children's literature, including the best-selling memoir *Always Running: La Vida Loca, Gang Days in L.A.* He lives in San Fernando, California.

Richard Blanco, the fifth U.S. Presidential Inaugural Poet, is the author of three collections of poetry, *City of a Hundred Fires, Directions to the Beach of the Dead, Looking for the Gulf Motel*, and a memoir, *The Prince of Los Cocuyos: A Miami Childhood*. He lives in Bethel, Maine.

FURTHER INFORMATION

Our Little Roses Home & Sponsorship:
www.ourlittleroses.org

Annual poetry fellowship to Our Little Roses:
www.olrpfellowship.com

Documentary:
www.voicesbeyondthewallmovie.com

Tia Chucha's Centro Cultural & Bookstore
and Tia Chucha Press:
www.tiachucha.org